Science Technology Engineering Math
STEM STARTERS FOR KIDS

STEM GREEN SCIENCE AT HOME

FUN ENVIRONMENTAL SCIENCE PROJECTS TO HELP KIDS SAVE THE EARTH

- **IN THE KITCHEN** pages 2 to 15
- **IN YOUR ROOM** pages 16 to 25
- **IN THE BATHROOM** pages 26 to 35
- **OUTDOORS** pages 36 to 47
- **WORDS TO KNOW** page 48

written by Susan Martineau · designed and illustrated by Vicky Barker
Science advisor: Georgina Durrant

for YOUNG READERS

Text and illustrations copyright © b small publishing 2021 • First Racehorse for Young Readers Edition 2021 • All rights reserved. No part of this book may be reproduced in any manner without the express written consent of the publisher, except in the case of brief excepts in critical reviews or articles. All inquiries should be addressed to Racehorse for Young Readers, 307 West 36th Street, 11th Floor, New York, NY 10018. • Racehorse for Young Readers books may be purchased in bulk at special discounts for sales promotions, corporate gifts, fund-raising or education purposes. Special editions can also be created to specifications. For details, contact the Special Sales Department at Skyhorse Publishing, 307 West 36th Street, 11th Floor, New York, NY 10018 or info@skyhorsepublishing.com. • Racehorse for Young Readers is a pending trademark of Skyhorse Publishing, Inc.®, a Delaware corporation. • Visit our website at skyhorsepublishing.com • 10 9 8 7 6 5 4 3 2 1 • ISBN: 978-1-63158-660-6 •
Production: Madeleine Ehm • Publisher: Sam Hutchinson • Art director: Vicky Barker • Science education consultant: Georgina Durrant • Printed in China

Green Science in the Kitchen

Scientists learn about the world around us by doing experiments and investigations. You can be a scientist, too. The green science experiments in this book will help you to understand how our planet is changing.

The kitchen experiments in this part of the book use everyday things you probably have at home already, but don't forget to ask a grown-up before using them. You can also reuse all kinds of things from clean plastic food containers to old jam jars. Read through the whole experiment to make sure you have everything you need before you begin.

REUSE!
Make a handy notebook out of scrap paper and old envelopes. Punch some holes and tie the sheets together with old string or ribbon. Draw or write up your experiments like a real scientist. Make up your own experiments, too.

BE SAFE!
Ask a grown-up to stand by, especially when you are heating or cutting things.

Climate Change

The climate on our planet is getting hotter and hotter, and humans are making it worse. We burn **fossil fuels** (oil, gas, and coal) to power cars and to make electricity. These fuels give off a harmful gas called **carbon dioxide**. This gas traps the Sun's heat in Earth's atmosphere and is making our planet heat up like a greenhouse. We need to use other ways to power our planet.

BUT it is not too late. We can ALL do something to help.

Always clean up after your experiments!

Be an eco-hero!

Eco-tip

Make a Green Diary and keep a note of something you do to help the planet every week. There are lots of ideas in this book.

Words to Know

Special science words in **bold** are explained on page 48.

Kitchen
3

Melting Ice Cap

As the temperature on Earth rises, the frozen seawater of the world's coldest oceans is melting. Frozen ice sheets on land are melting, too. Make your very own ice cap to see what happens when this ice melts.

1. Pour some water into a shallow plastic food container. Add a couple of drops of food coloring and stir.

2. Put the container in the freezer for a few hours or overnight.

3. Place a few large stones in a large shallow dish. Pour in some water, but make sure the tops of the stones are above it.

4. Take the frozen ice cap out of its plastic container. Put it in the large dish on top of the container. Watch what happens!

Kitchen

4

How It Works – Let's Take a Closer Look!

The ice slowly melts and the level of the water in the dish rises. You can see the water coming further up the stones. It might even cover some of them. The same thing is happening on our planet. Water that is frozen **solid** as ice caps on the land is melting as the climate warms up. The **liquid** water then makes the level of the seas and oceans go up. Places that are on coasts or islands are in danger of being flooded and covered by water, just like the stones in your experiment.

The ice cap might slither off the plastic container as it melts!

Did You Know?

Trees take in and store **carbon dioxide**. **Carbon dioxide** is one of the **greenhouse gases** that are heating our climate. Rainforests on the planet are being cut down to make room for growing crops, grazing animals and to use the wood from the trees. We need these forests to protect our planet.

Eco-tip

Plant a tree! Perhaps you can set up a tree-planting team at school. Trees are super eco-heroes!

Kitchen

Waterworks

When we turn on our taps out comes lovely, clean water. Before it reaches us, water has to be cleaned to get rid of bugs and dirt. You can do an experiment to see how water is filtered to get rid of dirt.

1. Mix some soil and water in a jug.

2. Put a piece of kitchen towel into a sieve or funnel.

3. Hold the sieve or funnel over another jug and slowly pour the dirty water into it.

How It Works – Let's Take a Closer Look!

The kitchen towel acts as a **filter**. It lets the water through, but stops most of the soil and dirt. It separates the **solid** dirt from the **liquid** water. Our drinking water is filtered through gravel and sand at water treatment works to get rid of dirt. Special cleaning chemicals are also used to kill any harmful germs that might make us ill. Water treatment works use energy to clean our water and also to pump it to our houses. This makes it very important not to waste a drop!

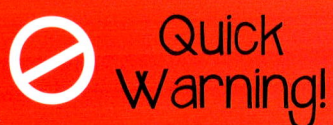

Quick Warning!

Your filtered water is not safe for you to drink, but plants will love it.

Eco-tip

Be a water leak detective! You can check your home and school for any dripping taps or water leaks that are wasting water. Ask for them to be fixed!

Did You Know?

Drinking tap water in most countries is very safe and it is also best for the planet. Transporting bottled water to the shops uses fuel that makes harmful **greenhouse gases**. Plastic bottles are also made out of **fossil fuels**.

I'm going to use this reusable bottle instead of buying a plastic one!

Kitchen

7

Recycling Counts

Every day humans throw lots of stuff away. Too much garbage ends up in massive dumps called landfill sites. We need to think about everything we put in the trash can. Can it be reused or recycled instead? Ask your family to help with this garbage experiment.

1. Design and draw a chart. You can reuse old card and paper for this. Make a different column for each type of garbage that can be recycled.

2. Ask everyone in your family to make a mark for each piece of garbage they put in your recycling bins.

3. After a week, you can add up the totals for each column.

Kitchen
8

How It Works – Let's Take a Closer Look!

Hopefully a lot of your family's garbage went into the recycling bins (and even a compost bin if you have one). Imagine if all of this stuff went straight to the dump instead. Recycling is very important. If we do not recycle, the planet will look like one big garbage dump. Lots of energy and materials will also be used to make new things when we could reuse what we already have. **Zero waste** means trying to make sure that nothing goes into landfill!

Avoid using things that you can only use once!

Eco-tip

Your house may already have some recycling bins. You could make some labels for them so everyone knows which bin to use. Make sure all the garbage you put in them is clean.

Science to the Rescue

Did you know that making one new aluminum drink can uses the same amount of energy as it takes to recycle 20 cans? Glass can be recycled over and over again. Card, paper, and food cartons can be recycled several times until, finally, they are made into toilet paper!

Kitchen
9

Plant Food

Some kitchen garbage can be made into tasty food for plants instead of throwing it in the trash can. This is a very slow experiment which takes a few weeks. You could note or draw what happens each week.

1. Make several holes in the bottom of a large, clean plastic bottle using a drawing-pin. Cut around the top section of the bottle. (Ask a grown-up to help.)

2. Stand the bottle in an old container or plastic dish. Put in a layer of soil from the garden or a houseplant.

3. Add some ripped-up paper or card. Then put in peels, apple cores, and teabags. Sprinkle with a little water.

4. Put the top of the bottle upside down like a funnel. Stand it in a warm place and cover the top with an old cloth.

5. Add waste to the bottle until it reaches the funnel. Stir the compost once a week.

vegetable and fruit peelings

teabags

apple cores

uncooked veg

Kitchen

10

Quick Warning!

Don't add cooked food or meat to your compost. Wash your hands carefully each time you add to and stir the compost.

Did You Know?

Artificial chemical fertilizerss can end up in lakes and rivers. They harm the creatures and plants that live there. Some **artificial** fertilizerss are made using **fossil fuels**, too. **Organic**, natural fertilizerss, like your plant food, are much better for the planet.

How It Works – Let's Take a Closer Look!

After a few days you can see the waste beginning to look very different. This is because tiny little organisms called **bacteria** feed on it. As they break the waste down it starts to sink lower in the bottle. It is **decomposing** and changing into natural, **organic** fertilizers which is full of **nutrients** for plants. It will take quite a few weeks for it to be ready as plant food, or compost, but it does start to look like muck quite quickly!

Eco-tip

When your compost is ready it will look and smell more like soil. You can then mix it into the soil for a pot plant or dig it into a flowerbed.

Chop banana skins into small pieces before adding them.

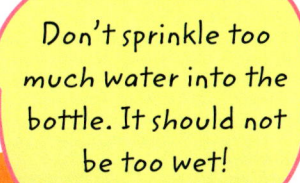

Don't sprinkle too much water into the bottle. It should not be too wet!

Then wash your paws!

Kitchen

No-package Popcorn

The next time you fancy a snack, how about making your own instead of opening a plastic packet? There won't be any packaging to throw away and you can also share it with your friends.

1. Weigh 50 g (2 oz) of popping corn. Put two teaspoons of vegetable oil in a large saucepan with a lid.

2. Heat the oil and add the corn. Put the lid on tightly.

3. Heat gently. Keep the lid firmly on the pan and shake the pan until the popping stops!

🚫 **Quick Warning!**
Ask a grown-up to stand by while you are cooking. Use oven gloves to hold the pan and lid.

Kitchen

Eco-tip

You could try making some other food like pizza, milkshakes, or yogurt. You will be helping the planet and you will know exactly what ingredients have gone into them, too!

Did You Know?

Making your own food is not only a way of avoiding plastic packaging that ends up in our garbage, it also saves on fuel being used to transport it from the snack factory to stores. The further your food has to travel to reach you, the more fuel is used to get it there and the more harmful **greenhouse gases** are sent out into Earth's atmosphere.

How It Works – Let's Take a Closer Look!

The pieces of corn, or kernels, heat up in the oil. Inside each little kernel there is a tiny drop of water. When the kernels heat up this also heats the water drop and turns it into a gas called **water vapor**. This builds **pressure** inside the kernel which makes the corn **expand** and grow so big that it POPS! The pan will look very full.

I like sprinkling mine with cinnamon and syrup!

Kitchen

Growing Food

Eating more vegetables is not just good for us, but also good for our planet! If you like, you can grow your own and you don't even need a garden to get started.

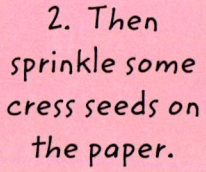

1. Put two or three layers of kitchen towel into a shallow, plastic food tray. Dampen them with water.

2. Then sprinkle some cress seeds on the paper.

3. Put in a warm, light place and keep the paper damp, but not too wet.

4. After a few days, cut the cress with scissors and eat it!

Kitchen

Eco-tip

You could buy seeds or small plants from a garden center or nursery to grow other food, too. Plant them in containers like yogurt pots, cracked bowls or baskets lined with plastic wrapping that you might otherwise throw away!

Did You Know?

There are more and more humans on Earth and we need lots of food to feed us all. The best way to make sure there will be enough to share is for us all to eat less red meat, like beef from cows. Fields where animals graze the grass need to be used for growing crops for us to eat instead.

burp! burp! burp!

Cows give off a bad greenhouse gas called methane, too!

How It Works – Let's Take a Closer Look!

The little seeds **germinate**, or sprout, within two days. (They might even germinate in 24 hours.) There is a store of food, or **nutrients**, in the seeds to feed the little shoots to start with. The shoots soon grow bigger and bigger and you will see little leaves appearing.

The seedlings now need light and water to help them make food for themselves and to grow. This food-making in plants is called **photosynthesis**.

Cress tastes delicious in sandwiches and salads!

Kitchen

15

Green Science in Your Room

Your room is like your own mini-world. You can make it as "green" as you like! These experiments are just to get you started. You can make up your own investigations, just like a real scientist. Write up what happens or draw the results.

These experiments use things you will probably have at home already and lots of things you can reuse. Check with a grown-up before using them, and read through the whole experiment before you begin to make sure you have everything you need.

REUSE! Make a science kit using an old box so that you always have your notebook and equipment handy.

Clean up your room when you've finished!

QUICK WARNING! Never play with the electrical sockets in your room.

Bedroom
16

Polluted Planet

Humans are polluting the air, water, and land of Earth with all kinds of dirty and harmful things. We make garbage that gets dumped in the ground or in the seas. We burn fuels that make the air filthy and we use poisonous chemicals that get into rivers and oceans. We even use so many lights at night that the sky is not properly dark any more. We need to clean up!

BUT it's not too late! More and more countries are using green energy like wind and solar power.

Set up an Eco-hero Club with your friends!

Eco-tip
Make wrapping paper, cards and envelopes with old bits of paper and card.

Words to Know
Special science words in **bold** are explained on page 48.

Bedroom

17

Sort Your Stuff

Most of us have lots of stuff in our rooms, but do you know what all your toys, gadgets, and clothes are made from? Have a look at some of them and see if you can work it out.

1. Copy this chart on to a large piece of card or paper.

PAPER	PLASTIC	WOOL
notebook box	phone	sweater socks

COTTON	METAL	WOOD
T-shirt jeans	phone lamp	drawers

2. Draw or write the names of your things next to the materials shown. Some things are made out of more than one material.

Bedroom

18

Science to the Rescue

Many plastics made out of **fossil fuels** are very hard to recycle. It is even more difficult if they are mixed with other materials. Scientists and inventors are experimenting with new sorts of plastic made out of materials including mushrooms, palm leaves and shellfish shells.

Eco-tip

Have a Swap Party! You and your friends can swap things that you do not want any more instead of buying new things. Perhaps you can swap with a friend to get a T-shirt you've always liked!

How It Works - Let's Take a Closer Look!

Some things are made out of materials that will run out one day. These are called **non-renewable** resources. They include **fossil fuels** and metals. Plastic is made out of oil, a **fossil fuel**. Some clothes are made of fabrics like polyester and nylon. These are also made from **fossil fuels**. Metals, like steel, aluminum and gold, are also **non-renewable**. Some of our favourite gadgets are made using these.

Renewable materials can be grown, or made, over and over again. These include wool from sheep, wood from trees, paper (made from trees), and cotton which grows on plants.

We need to recycle and reuse things as much as possible!

Bedroom

19

Lights Out!

There are so many lights blazing in our cities and towns that the skies above them are never really dark. It is hard to see any stars. This light **pollution** is causing problems for many of the animals on our planet. Find a torch to do this experiment.

1. Make your room as dark as you can. Then shine the torch at the wall.

2. Now cut a piece of card so that it is the right size to wrap around the end of the torch like a tube. (Put your room light on while you do this!)

3. Fix the card around the torch with some reusable sticky tack.

4. Turn off the room light and shine the torch at the wall again. Can you see a difference in the way the light works?

Bedroom

"An old toilet paper roll tube might fit the end of your torch!"

"Try star-spotting in town and also the countryside. Where can you see the most stars?"

How It Works – Let's Take a Closer Look!

When you put the card or tube around the end of the torch, the beam of light does not spread out as far as it did without it. The card acts like a shield and makes the area smaller and narrower. Streetlights can be designed in the same way so that they only light a small area instead of spreading light into the night sky. This helps to control what is called **sky glow** from lights.

Eco-tip

Turn lights off before leaving a room and remind other people as well! You could also check that your school does not have unnecessary lights on when no one is there.

Did You Know?

Light pollution confuses **nocturnal** creatures who come out at night to hunt or find food. Baby turtles use the bright horizon over the ocean to find their way to safety in the water, but they head the wrong way towards the bright lights of towns near their hatching beaches.

Bedroom

21

Wrap Up!

When the weather is cold and the heating is on, it is important not to waste the energy that makes our heaters and radiators work. We can do an experiment to see how to keep warm!

1. Pour some warm water into two glass jam jars with lids. (Ask a grown-up to help with this to make sure the water is not too hot.)

2. Put the lids on the jars. Wrap one jar in a scarf or wool sweater and leave the other one unwrapped.

3. After 30 minutes put your finger in the water in each jar. Is there a difference between them? Write down what you have found out.

Bedroom

My fur keeps me warm!

How It Works – Let's Take a Closer Look!

The water in the jar wrapped in the scarf or jumper kept warmer than the water in the unwrapped jar. This is because the scarf or jumper stopped a lot of the heat from leaving the jar. It made a layer of **insulation** that slowed the **conduction** of the heat. (It is a bit like you sleeping under a duvet instead of completely uncovered.)

Houses need **insulation**, too. Pipes and storage for heating and hot water need to be covered or made from insulating materials to keep in the heat for as long as possible. If your house is well insulated, it does not use as much energy to heat it and keep it warm.

Eco-tip

Close your curtains and stop drafts from coming under the door to keep your room warm when it is cold outside. Wear an extra layer if you are cold, instead of turning up the heating!

Science to the Rescue

Insulation for buildings can be made from some very planet-friendly materials. Cellulose **insulation** is made from recycled newspapers and wool **insulation** comes from sheep!

Bedroom

23

Bedroom Rainforest

Trees can make it rain! This very green experiment shows you how trees and plants pump water into the air to help make clouds. You'll need a pot plant that fits on your windowsill for this.

1. Put a large plastic bag over a leafy potted plant.

2. Use old ribbon or string to tie the bag around the stems. Leave the soil uncovered.

3. Put the pot in an old plastic dish or on a saucer. Keep the soil moist and leave for a few days.

How It Works – Let's Take a Closer Look!

After a few hours you will see the bag beginning to mist up inside. After a couple of days droplets of water appear on the inside of the bag. Plants soak up water to make food for themselves and some of this water is 'breathed out' by the plant through its leaves in the form of a gas called **water vapor**. This gas then turns back (**condenses**) into liquid water. This is a process called **transpiration**. In tropical rainforests, the trees release so much **water vapor** that they make their own rainclouds.

Never put a plastic bag near your face.

A cactus garden does not need much water!

Did You Know?

We must save our planet's rainforests. Trees not only soak up harmful **carbon dioxide** gas, but they also produce the gas we need to stay alive. The Amazon rainforest provides one fifth (20%) of the **oxygen** humans need to breathe.

Eco-tip

Take the bag off and keep the plant in your room after you've done the experiment. It will help to clean up the air while you are sleeping!

Bedroom

25

Green Science in the Bathroom

You can do green science experiments in your bathroom, especially as these investigations all have to do with water! Note or draw your results just like a real scientist. You could also make up your own experiments.

You don't need any special equipment. The experiments use or reuse things you probably already have at home. Don't forget to ask a grown-up before using them and, before you begin, always read through the whole experiment to make sure you have everything you need.

REUSE!
For some of these experiments you will need a chart to write on. You can make one using old card or cardboard and bits of string or ribbon. Hang it on the bathroom door.

Be careful when you run a hot tap or shower to make sure the water is not too hot!

Water on Earth

Humans use lots of fresh water and it is there for us because of an amazing process called the water cycle. Rain and snow fall to Earth. The Sun heats the water in Earth's oceans, lakes, and rivers. Water then **evaporates** and becomes a gas called **water vapor**. It rises up and cools down. As it cools, it turns back into water (**condenses**) and makes clouds. Then it rains or snows again! The hotter climate on our planet is changing the pattern of our weather, where it rains, and how often. This will affect our fresh water supplies in the future.

Eco-tip

Try to use natural products in the bathroom to avoid lots of harmful chemicals that end up in our rivers and seas.

We can all do something to save water!

Eco-heroes to the rescue!

Words to Know

Special science words in **bold** are explained on page 48.

🚫 BE SAFE!

Never play with the medicines or cleaning chemicals you might have in your bathroom.

Bathroom

27

Water Waster

Even though we have huge oceans of saltwater on our planet, there is not much fresh water on Earth. We really need to use what we have carefully. You can do this experiment the next time you clean your teeth.

1. Put a large bowl or plastic container in the sink.

2. Turn on the tap and clean your teeth!

3. Use a jug to measure how much water you have used.

Bathroom

How It Works – Let's Take a Closer Look!

The amount of water you have measured depends on how well you clean your teeth! But you will see that it uses a lot of water when you keep a tap running. If you switch off the tap after wetting your toothbrush you will save this water from going straight down the drain! Water covers about two thirds of the planet, but there is only a tiny amount of FRESH water for us to use. It is like having 100 cups of water and only being able to drink three of them.

Use the water you have measured to water the garden or house plants.

I've got a wooden toothbrush to avoid plastic ones!

Eco-tip

Find out where you can send old toothbrushes and toothpaste tubes to be recycled. You could collect them with your friends and send them off.

Science to the Rescue

Salty water from our seas and oceans is made into fresh, drinking water in many countries. This is called **desalination** as it takes the salt out of the water. But it uses a lot of energy, often made by power stations using **fossil fuels**, to do this.

Bathroom
29

Water Power

We need to use other ways of powering our planet to avoid burning **fossil fuels**. These make gases that are heating our planet like a greenhouse. Another way to make energy is to use the power of water.

1. Cut a circle from an old plastic lid. Make a hole in the middle big enough for a straw to fit through. (Ask a grown-up to help.)

2. Carefully cut slits all around the lid. Bend the flaps so that they are out of line with each other.

3. Put a paper straw through the hole. Keep it in place with some sticky tack on each side.

4. Put a wooden or metal skewer through the straw and then hold your water wheel under a running cold tap!

Bathroom

30

How It Works – Let's Take a Closer Look!

As you hold the water wheel under the tap it whizzes round really fast. The wheel is turned by the power of the running water. The power of water can be used to make **hydroelectricity**. Dams are built across rivers and lakes and the water turns turbines which make the electricity. No harmful **greenhouse gases** are made, but the dams can affect people and animals who live nearby.

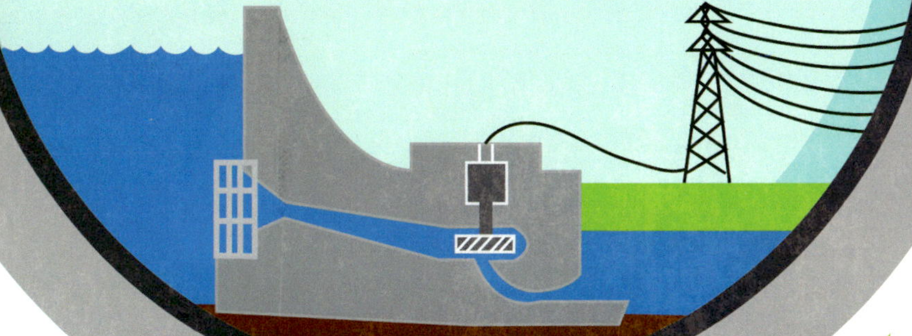

Keep the plug in so you don't waste the water!

Science to the Rescue

Power from water is a kind of **renewable** energy which will not run out. Another form of **renewable** energy is wind power. Huge wind turbines use the force of the wind to make electricity. It is a clean way to power the planet which does not make damaging **greenhouse gases** like **carbon dioxide**.

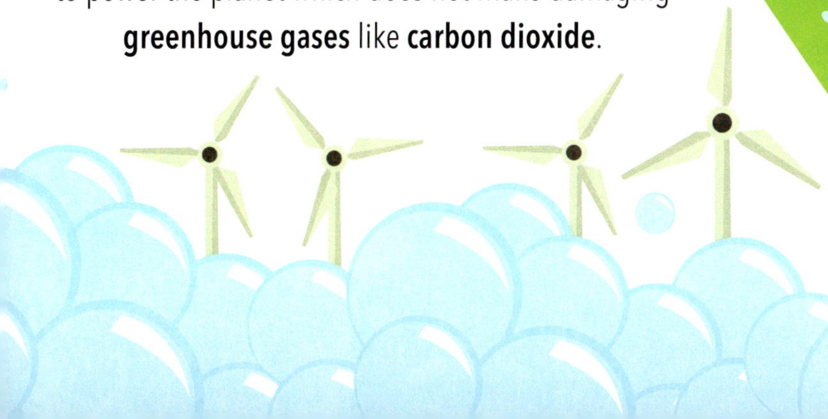

Eco-tip

Clean, old squeeze bottles make super-soaking squirters for outdoors. Use the water from the sink after you've done this experiment!

Bathroom

31

Sparkling Sinks

It is important to keep our bathrooms clean, but some of the chemicals in cleaning products are not very good for us or the **environment**. Luckily, it is really easy to make your own much safer products.

1. Mix three heaped tablespoons of baking soda with two tablespoons of water. Mix well to make a paste.

2. Wet a reusable cloth or rag. Put some of the paste in the sink and scrub! Use rubber gloves if your skin is sensitive to baking soda.

3. You can also use the paste to clean the taps. Rinse the basin with water and wipe with a dry cloth.

Bathroom

Eco-tip

Cut up old T-shirts to make handy cleaning cloths. Old toothbrushes are great for scrubbing around taps!

Did You Know?

The paste made with baking soda is a safe, natural way of cleaning because it does not include lots of harmful chemicals that can hurt us and the **environment** when they are flushed down the drain.

How It Works – Let's Take a Closer Look!

When you mix the baking soda with the water it makes a natural cleaning mixture that dissolves dirt and grease. The paste is also a bit gritty so it is good for scrubbing sinks! The baking soda is an **alkali**. This is the opposite of an **acid** (such as vinegar or lemon juice). Nasty smells are often **acidic** so the **alkali** bicarbonate is also good at getting rid of them, too.

I like using an old sock to do my cleaning!

Wash your hands after cleaning.

Bathroom
33

Shower Time

This experiment is a competition! It will not only get everyone in your family thinking about how much water is used every time they have a nice, hot shower, but also about how much electricity is used.

1. Make a Shower Chart with some old card. Hang it up on the bathroom door with a pencil at the ready.

2. Ask everyone in your family to time themselves each time they take a shower. Use a kitchen timer or the clock on a phone.

3. See who can have the quickest one, but still get properly clean!

How It Works – Let's Take a Closer Look!

"Perhaps your electricity comes from a solar panel on your roof?"

"It is still best not to waste it!"

Every time you take a hot shower it uses energy in the form of electricity to heat the water. Some showers also have pumps that use electricity, too. The shorter your shower, the less energy you use. You also save water of course. See if you can have showers that only take about four minutes. This will help save electricity and water.

Science to the Rescue

Water that has been used in the home, except water from toilets, is called grey water. It can be filtered and cleaned so that it can be reused for flushing toilets, watering gardens, or in washing machines.

Eco-tip

Keep a bucket in the shower to catch the clean water while you wait for it to warm up! You can use it later to wash your hands.

Bathroom
35

Green Science Outdoors

Scientists do lots of experiments and investigations outdoors and you can, too! You can do these experiments in a garden, on a balcony, or in the park. Write down or draw what happens when you do the experiments, just like a real scientist.

You don't need any special equipment as you can use, and reuse, things you probably already have at home. Don't forget to ask a grown-up before using them. Before you begin, always read through the whole experiment to make sure you have everything you need.

REUSE!
You could use some old card and paper to make an outdoor science folder for your notes and sketches.

Wash your hands when you've finished outside.

🚫 BE SAFE!
Ask a grown-up before you go out into the garden and never go to the park on your own.

Animals in Danger

Biodiversity means all the great variety of living things that live on Earth. They all need to live in balance with each other, including humans. Too many animals and plants are dying out, or becoming **extinct**, because humans are destroying their homes by chopping down forests or polluting the land, sea, and air with garbage and nasty chemicals. We need to look after Earth for all of its amazing creatures, trees, and plants — not just for ourselves.

BUT it is not too late to help. Even taking small actions will make a difference.

Be an eco-hero and tell everyone else to be one, too!

Eco-tip
Do a litter-pick with your friends and family. Recycle as much of the garbage as you can.

Words to Know
Special science words in **bold** are explained on page 48.

Outdoors

37

Pesky Plastics

We all use things made out of plastic every day. And we often only use them once before throwing them away. Too much plastic is ending up in our oceans and seas, but how does this garbage spread so far and wide?

1. Slowly pour some water into one of the egg cups of an egg box. Keep pouring until each egg cup is full.

2. Now sprinkle some dry soil into one of the cups. Stir it with a stick.

3. Watch what happens to the soil.

Outdoors

38

How It Works – Let's Take a Closer Look!

The water flows easily from one egg cup to the other in the same way that water flows between the rivers and oceans on Earth. When you add the soil, this spreads across the egg cups, too. This is what happens when harmful pollution, like plastics, ends up in rivers and oceans. The movement of water, or currents, spreads the plastics across the oceans. In some places there are huge plastic islands of garbage far out to sea.

Plastic in the oceans hurts or kills sea creatures.

They eat plastic bags and old balloons because they think they are food.

Eco-tip

Can you think of ways to avoid plastic things that you only use once? You could make home-made decorations instead of plastic party balloons? It is more fun, too!

Science to the Rescue

Scientists are testing a way of collecting up plastic in the oceans using a huge floating barrier to scoop it up.

Outdoors

Oil Spill

Oil is used to make energy in power stations and gas for cars. It is transported all over the world in huge tankers and pipelines. Sometimes it spills into the seas and oceans and this is deadly for seabirds. Find some feathers in the garden or park to do this oily experiment.

1. Half-fill an old plastic container with water. Put a feather on it. What does it do?

2. Take the feather out. Pour about two tablespoons of vegetable oil on to the water.

3. Put the feather back in and swish it around. What happens now?

How It Works – Let's Take a Closer Look!

When you first put the feather on top of the water it floats. This is because birds have their own special kind of oil on their feathers. It stops feathers from getting soaked in the rain or on the sea. They **repel** water like a waterproof coat. But when you put the feather in the water with the vegetable oil it clogs up the feather and it does not float as well.

This is what happens to seabirds if they get fuel oil on their feathers. Fuel oil is thicker and stickier than vegetable oil. The poor birds get more and more covered in it as they struggle to take off from the oily sea surface and they often swallow the poisonous oil, too.

Electric cars do not use petrol or diesel!

Eco-tip

Walk or cycle to school instead of going in a car or bus if you can. This avoids using any petrol or diesel, which are made from oil.

Did You Know?

Oil has a kind of stretchy skin around it. Detergents, like dish soap liquid, can break up the skin around the drops of oil. Wildlife experts use detergents to clean seabirds, but only the strongest birds will survive.

Outdoors

Melt-down

As the climate warms up it is very important to find ways of keeping the planet cool. The ice and snow at the North and South Poles of our planet act like air-conditioning for Earth. This experiment shows you why. You need a sunny day for this experiment.

1. You need two clear plastic containers, a piece of white cardstock, and a piece of black cardstock.

2. Take them outside along with some ice cubes. Find a sunny spot.

3. Put an ice cube in each container. Place one on the white card and one on the black. Watch what happens.

Outdoors

42

How It Works – Let's Take a Closer Look!

The ice cubes melt in the heat of the sunshine. They change from **solid** to **liquid**. BUT the ice cube in the container above the white cardstock does not melt as quickly as the one placed above the black cardstock. The color white bounces back (**reflects**) most of the sunlight. Black soaks up (**absorbs**) light and heat, like a sponge soaks up water. This is why the ice cube above the white cardstock melts more slowly.

The huge WHITE sheets of ice at the North and South Poles of Earth **reflect** the heat of the Sun. They help to cool the climate so it is very important to stop them from melting.

Have a nice cool drink with the rest of the ice cubes while you watch!

Eco-tip

When it is hot outside you can keep your room as cool as possible by keeping the windows and curtains (or blinds) shut during the day.

Science to the Rescue

We can get power from the Sun. It is called **solar power** and is a **renewable** type of energy. This means that it will not run out like oil, coal, and gas. It does not put harmful gases into the atmosphere so it is much better for the planet. Solar panels are made of material that **absorbs** energy from the Sun and uses it to make electricity.

Outdoors

Night Hunt

You need to go out after dark to do this experiment in a garden or the park. Ask a grown-up to go with you. They can perhaps carry a drink or snack for you!

1. Hang a white sheet over a tree branch, clothesline or fence.

2. Shine a strong torch on the sheet so it lights up as much of it as possible.

3. Have a look at the moths (and other insects!) that land on the sheet.

Outdoors

44

How It Works – Let's Take a Closer Look!

Moths are attracted to the light and the white of the sheet. Most moths fly at night which makes them **nocturnal**, or night-time, creatures. They will also fly to sweet-smelling, night-flowering plants, too (especially if they are white). They help to **pollinate** plants when they move from one flower to another to feed. During the day, they sleep in sheltered places, like under leaves and on fences. Don't wake them up!

Moths have feathery feelers and butterflies have long, thin ones!

While you are waiting you can listen quietly for any other night creatures, like hedgehogs grunting!

Half a melon makes a good insect café.

Eco-tip
Make a Bug Buffet for creatures who might visit your garden or schoolyard. Piles of old leaves and branches make great homes for wildlife, too.

Did You Know?
Moths are called an **indicator species** which means they show us how healthy our **environment** is. They are easily affected by changes in climate and pollution. The more moths we see, the better!

Outdoors

Dirty Rain

When coal and gas are burned in factories, power stations, and cars they send harmful gases into the air. These not only warm up Earth's atmosphere, but also make rain dirty. See what happens when this rain falls on trees and plants.

1. Pick some sprigs with leaves on them.

2. Fill an old jam jar with vinegar. Put the sprigs into the jar.

3. Leave for a few days and note down what happens.

Outdoors

46

How It Works – Let's Take a Closer Look!

You begin to see the veins of the leaves going brown first. By the next day the leaves are curled and most of them are completely brown. The vinegar is an **acid**. In this experiment the vinegar plays the part of rain that has been made into **acid rain** by harmful gases.

Acid rain harms the leaves of trees and plants. Then they cannot collect light and **carbon dioxide** to make food for trees and plants. Too much **acid** soaking into soil also means that plants will not grow. Whole forests can be killed in this way.

The energy wasted by gadgets on standby is called vampire energy!

Don't breathe in the gas that comes off this!

Did You Know?

Acid rain also damages the brick and stone of buildings. If you put a piece of chalk into some vinegar you can see how this happens. This experiment is definitely best done outside!

Eco-tip

Turn off gadgets and chargers when you are not using them. Computers and TVs left on standby waste electricity which makes more harmful gases to warm up the world.

Outdoors

Green Words to Know

Absorb - When a material or surface soaks up a liquid. Sponges absorb water.

Acid - A substance that has a sour taste, like vinegar or lemon juice is **acidic**. Strong acids can 'burn'. **Acid rain** damages the natural environment and buildings.

Alkali - A substance that is the opposite of an acid but can be just as damaging. Alkalis often feel a bit soapy, like chalk.

Artificial - This describes something made by humans, instead of being found or growing naturally.

Bacteria - Tiny, invisible living things. Some are very helpful and break down dead stuff. Some bacteria can cause diseases. (**Bacterium** is the word for one.)

Biodiversity - The huge variety of living things on our planet.

Carbon dioxide - A gas made when fossil fuels are burnt to make energy. It is also the gas our bodies breathe out and trees take in.

Condenses - This means to change from a gas into a liquid. Water vapor, or steam, changes into drops of water when it touches something cold.

Conduction - One of the ways in which heat (or electricity) flows from one thing to another.

Decomposes - When something rots away.

Desalination - A way of taking the salt out of seawater.

Environment - The air, water or land that people, animals and plants live in or on.

Evaporate - When a liquid turns into a gas, usually when the liquid is heated.

Expand - To grow bigger or spread out.

Extinct - Animal and plant species are extinct when not a single one of them is left alive anywhere in the world.

Filter - A way of separating solids from a liquid.

Fossil fuels These are oil, coal and gas. They are natural fuels formed millions of years ago from dead animals and plants.

Germinate - When a seed sends out its first shoot. It uses nutrients inside the seed as food to start growing.

Greenhouse gases - Gases in the atmosphere that absorb energy from the Sun. They include carbon dioxide, methane and water vapor. Human activity makes and releases huge amounts of carbon dioxide into the atmosphere.

Hydroelectricity - A type of power made using the force of water to turn turbines to make electricity.

Indicator species - An animal or plant that is easily affected by changes in the environment, including pollution. Monitoring them is a useful clue to understand these changes.

Insulation - Materials that stop heat being conducted (**conduction**). They help to keep things hot or cold.

Liquid - Water is a liquid. Liquids can be poured and do not have a shape of their own.

Nocturnal - Describes a creature that mainly comes out at night.

Non-renewable - Means that once something is all used up there is no more of it and we cannot make any more. Non-renewable energy comes from fossil fuels. These will run out one day.

Nutrients - The foodstuff that plants or animals need to grow well. Plants get nutrients from the soil.

Organic - This means something made from living things. Organic fertilizers is made using animal poo (manure) or vegetable matter (compost).

Oxygen - A gas in the atmosphere that humans and many living things need to breathe. Trees produce oxygen.

Photosynthesis - The way that plants and trees use sunlight, water and carbon dioxide to make food for themselves.

Pollinate - When pollen is carried from one flower to another to fertilize it so that new plants will grow. Insects, like moths, are very important pollinators.

Pollution - When the air, water or land is damaged or made dirty by waste or harmful chemicals.

Pressure - When something pushes or presses down or against something else. It is a kind of force.

Reflects - When light is bounced off a surface. Sunlight reflects off white ice sheets.

Renewable - This means something that does not run out or can be grown again. Renewable energy comes from the Sun, wind or water.

Repel - When something acts as a barrier or pushes something away. A waterproof jacket is made of material that repels rain.

Sky glow - This is light pollution over our towns and cities. Too many lights make the night sky bright instead of dark.

Solar power - This is a way of making power by turning sunlight into electricity.

Solid - Solid things, like ice, have a shape of their own.

Transpiration - When plants take up water through their roots and give off water vapor through tiny holes in their leaves.

Water vapor - Water in the form of a gas. Steam and mist are water vapor.

Zero waste - This means sending no garbage and waste to landfill sites or dumps.